thirst
seeking God when all seems lost

christian bosse

Copyright © 2018 Christian Bosse
All rights reserved solely by the author. The author guarantees all contents are original and do not infringe upon the legal rights of any other person or work. No part of this publication may be reproduced without prior permission from the author.

Scripture quotations referenced NIV are taken from the Holy Bible, New International Version®, NIV®. Copyright © 1973, 1978, 1984, 2011 by Biblica, Inc.™ Used by permission of Zondervan. All rights reserved worldwide.
www.zondervan.com The "NIV" and "New International Version" are trademarks registered in the United States Patent and Trademark Office by Biblica, Inc.™

Printed in the United States of America
Cover illustration: Christian Bosse
Cover design: Christian Bosse

ISBN-13: 978-1723946585

other books by christian bosse

poetry

Sojourner
Rhythms of Rebirth

nonfiction

Arise With Singing
Arise With Singing: Study Guide

Hi,

Friend, this book was written for you. If you feel like you're lost in the midst of chaos, this book was written for you. If you feel like your soul is dried up and in desperate need of water, this book was written for you. If you feel like life has pushed you down and the people around you are just watching it unfold, this book was written for you.

This book was founded in the Word of God and in times of prayer. It was written for the children of God, man and woman alike, to know there is a Source that never runs out.

You will be encouraged by this book. You will be challenged by this book. You might even be offended by this book. Take each poem, prose, and letter from God with a grain of salt. Study the words, for they were carefully chosen. If you come across something you do not understand, look it up. If you read a verse that sticks out, go study it in depth. The deeper you dig into this book, the more you'll gain from it. It is not the end-all-be-all to growing in faith. (God and His Word come before any and all other written works, including this one.) No, this book is not all you need to grow as a Christ-follower, but it is a resource for you to expand your mind and begin the process of feasting on the wisdom of God.

I pray you read this book and see God and yourself in a new light. I pray you feel empowered and transformed by what you read. No matter what is happening around you, God is for you.

Immerse yourself in this book. I pray you won't regret it.

– c.bosse

thirst

"As the deer pants for streams of water,
so my soul pants for you, my God.
My soul thirsts for God, for the living God.
When can I go and meet with God?"

Psalm 42:1-2 NIV

christian bosse

When is the last time you were truly thirsty for God?

thirst

God is never exhausted of chasing us down. It is a tireless pursuit. He never grows weary.

Learn to match His fervor. May you never be exhausted chasing after Him. Run Him down, meeting Him halfway in an embrace.

christian bosse

You uncover every stone
and peek behind every tree.
You look under every rug
and behind every curtain.
You are anxious to find a fix.

God is the only well
that can quench your thirst.
His well never runs dry.

thirst

Find joy in the secret place.
Find peace in the dwelling place.
His freedom is found at the altar.
His wisdom is found on holy ground.

christian bosse

"Learn to still your heart and mind. Settle down into My presence. I am the I am."

thirst

Practice the discipline of stillness. Silence your heart and mind. Open your spiritual ears to the whispers of the Holy Spirit. Take note of what He has to say.

christian bosse

Panting, I long
for your love.
It seems gone.
I feel a tug
in a direction. I do not know
where I am headed
or where I am to go.
I'm trying not to discredit
this feeling inside of me.
It's a kind of yearning
that's guiding me.
Slowly, I'm learning
that if I don't find
what I need
my heart, soul, and mind
will choose to feed
on what's not lovely or pure.
Oh, how I need You.
Lord, I need Your cure.

thirst

The ways of this world will never truly satisfy your soul. It might wet your whistle, but it will never fill your body with the hydration it needs to continue on.

Your soul is thirsty, yet, you fill it with the temporary fixes of this world. The material entertainments of life here on earth are like a homemade pitcher of punch. Though tasty, the punch is made of sugars and syrups and synthetic dyes, none of which have the ability to truly hydrate your soul.

Put down your plastic cups of temporary sustenance. Pick up an ice-cold glass of water and drink. This is what you need to survive.

thirst

We are made of
water. Yet, we fill
ourselves up on other
things. It's as if we do not
know who we are or what
compromises our bodies. We
neglect instead of nurture, hinder
instead of healing. We'd rather waste our
time on what we want instead of what we
truly need. Perhaps now is the time we change
our minds and remember who we really are.

christian bosse

There is a fountain that never runs dry.
There is a bottomless well.
There is a river without an end.
There is an endless ocean.

thirst

Steady yourself in the arms of your heavenly Father. Find balance in the Holy Spirit. The world around you might be a chaotic whirlpool, but the presence of the Lord is your lifeboat to safely sail you through the storm. Cling to His presence with all you've got.

The water has been shut off for quite some time. The pipes are all dried up. You pull at each faucet, begging the water to stream down. Your heart races as you begin to realize that there is no water left in your home. Quickly, your mind pieces together a plan. You grab your keys and bolt through the door. You'd go anywhere – everywhere – to find water.

"I am your Living Water. When you forget to pay the bill, the water dries up. The plumbing lulls a saddening hum because it hasn't a single drop left to give.

My child, run to Me. Search for Me with desperation. I am not far away. I am closer than you think. Choose to satisfy your thirst with My presence."

thirst

Don't wait until the bill is unpaid to search for living water.

christian bosse

Thirst, child.
Thirst.

For your lips are parched.
Your soul is dry.
Your body tells of your
thirstiness. But you live
as if your soul is quenched.

Drink up.
Have your fill.
And when you think you
    have had enough,
Drink again.

thirst

"My tears have been my food
    day and night,
while people say to me all day long,
    'Where is your God?'
These things I remember
    as I pour out my soul:
how I used to go to the house of God
    under the protection of the Mighty One
with shouts of joy and praise
    among the festive throng."

Psalm 42:3-4 NIV

christian bosse

Once upon a time, you carried a tune of joy. Your eyes were alight with gladness and your smile rarely diminished. You have now forgotten the happy song you once sang. Your eyes are filled with tears and your lips are tugged downward in a frown.

thirst

Without You there is no
    sky, no
    air, no
    breath
We are all just waxed
    figures, like
    statues, like
    monuments
telling stories of
    what was, or
    what could've been, a big
    what if
lost potential stuck in the balance asking
    who are we
    what are we to do
    how are we to do it
without You there is only
    silence, and
    stillness, and
    solitude

christian bosse

Oh, how deep
is the abyss.
I sit and wait
in uncertainty
not knowing how
I will be saved.
I no longer tilt
my head back
and gaze above.
I lean back and
wonder where
my help will
come from.

thirst

Fear and doubt are knocking on the door to your heart.
Will you answer?

christian bosse

Peace be still my
    heart
don't start
to race at the speed of
    light
A flight of
    fear, oh
    dear
heart of mine don't be
    afraid, or run
    away.
Run to God when all feels
    lost.

thirst

Jesus is the one who settles the stirring dust of my heart.

christian bosse

It is okay to feel sadness. It is okay to experience your emotions. Let them out. Set them free. Pour them out into your art. Deposit your mourning into your work.

In time, your pain can become a passionate masterpiece.

thirst

Take your tears
and mix them into
vessels of paint.
Dip your fingers
into the pigment.
Mark up your canvas.
Spill your emotions
all over the blank space,
creating a new work
of art full of depth
and sincerity.

christian bosse

Let your heart release the weight of what's stirring inside of you. Cast out your cares so they do not swallow you up. Though every tear is a small droplet into the bucket of your soul, it won't be long until the bucket is a burden to carry.

thirst

Lament.
Mourn.
Weep.

But don't let your heart settle into cynicism.

christian bosse

"Why, my soul, are you downcast?
   Why so disturbed within me?
Put your hope in God,
   for I will yet praise Him,
   my Savior and my God."

Psalm 42:5 NIV

thirst

"When you seek My face,
I will sustain you. I will
craft a recipe for break-
through. You will not go
hungry. You will feast
on the blessings I place
on your table."

christian bosse

Hold on to hope. No storm lasts forever.

thirst

Faith cannot exist without a question and an answer. The question is what we often focus on, causing ourselves to forget the joy we once had. Peace is erased from our minds. We lose sight of our identity.

The answer is always the same. It never fails or wavers. It doesn't buckle under pressure. It isn't diminished by fear. Though we often neglect to remember, the answer is continually faithful.

Jesus is the answer to our questions. He is the pioneer and perfecter of our faith.

christian bosse

Within you is the key to your destiny. It's often in use, yet rarely thought of. Your mouth determines the direction you will go. With it, you speak life or death. What words do you use to describe your life and your future?

thirst

Fill in the cracks of your heart and mind. Cover every nook and cranny that you can find. Stuff yourself with praise and hope. Leave no room for doubt to creep in.

christian bosse

The song you sing in your heart and mind determines the trajectory of your destiny. Will you fill your spirit with praise? Or will you stifle your dreams with the sounds of complaining?

thirst

When we hold on to our negative feelings, we plant weeds in the garden of our souls. The ugly shrubs multiply until we are nothing but bitterness.

Tend to your garden. Snuff out the negativity. Wage war on the weeds before they overtake your soul.

christian bosse

Your grumbling pollutes the air around you, making it difficult to breathe. Joy is snuffed out of the room. Vision is altered. Peace is no more.

Open a window. Praise the smog away. Clear the air with worship.

thirst

Learn to praise the Lord in the wilderness. Posture your heart for the promise awaiting you. Live in expectant hope, because your God is faithful. His goodness never ceases. It is unwavering. You can trust in the Lord because He is steadfast and persevering.

christian bosse

"My souls is downcast within me;
    therefore I will remember you
from the land of the Jordan,
    the heights of Hermon – from Mount Mizar.
Deep calls to deep
    in the roar of your waterfalls;
all your waves and breakers
    have swept over me."

Psalm 42:6-7 NIV

thirst

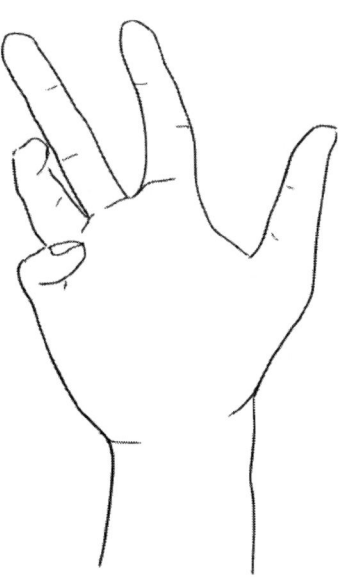

christian bosse

You feel as though you're sinking. You fear that you might drown. You look around, seeing nothing but water closing in on you. Though the waters rise as the tide rushes in, your God is helping you stay afloat.

"In times of trouble, remind yourself of My goodness. Like pictures in a photo album, sit and review the times I have provided for you. I have done it before. I will do it again. I am the unchanging God. I am the Good Father. I will not let you fall."

christian bosse

You feel broken,
like pieces of a once-treasured
vase shattered on the ground.
You think God has
drowned you in trouble
after trouble, turning a blind
eye to your situation.
You begin to believe
there is no way out.
You'll only continue to drown.
Fix your eyes above.
Your Savior is near.

God is not cruel. He does not bully His children. He doesn't pummel you down to nothing for fun. God is not cruel. He is on your side.

christian bosse

It is common to lash out when wounded. It's natural to bite the Hand that feeds you when you feel blindsided by your trials. It's easy to blame God for all that is happening. He is all-knowing and all-powerful. You quickly wonder why He didn't stop this from happening.

We do not know why trials and tribulations come our way, but we can trust that God isn't trying to cripple us.

In the midst of the confusion and heartbreak, turn to God. Long for His love and mercy. Don't push Him away out of frustration. Let Him heal your wounds and care for your bruises. He is a magnificent Father. He is for your good.

christian bosse

There is a type of longing that can only be satisfied by the depths of God's profound love. When you look deep into the eyes of the Father, you are staring into infinite beauty. He is not limited to the comprehension of our earthly minds. No. He is majestic in a way that can never truly be defined.

thirst

christian bosse

Though the waves crash over you, keep your head up. Hold your head above water. Tread to stay afloat. Do not give up. Gaze up at the sky knowing that the tide will falter any minute.

thirst

"Doubt,"
my heart shouts
as it looks around me
and sees only obstacles.

"Give up,"
my body cries out
as it begins to buckle
under the weight of the breakers.

"Reject Him,"
my ears hear a strangely
enticing voice whisper
in the background.

"Believe,"
my soul beckons,
calling me out of my
state of desperation.

christian bosse

Take a look at all that God has done for you. Relive the feeling of triumph. Repeat as necessary.

"By day the Lord directs His love,
   at night His song is with me –
   a prayer to the God of my life."

Psalm 42:8 NIV

christian bosse

You are covered in a thick blanket of serenity. The love of your Father is a pillow for your head at night.

Rest.
Rest.
Rest.

thirst

Stop what you're doing. Close your eyes. Thrust off your worries and listen. Do you hear it? Do you hear the melody? God is singing over you. Listen closely to the words He is singing. He is confident. Put your hope in Him.

christian bosse

Adored.
Treasured.
Cherished.
Embraced.
Loved.

You are His prize.

"You say you want more of Me. Well, here I am, my child. I am not hiding from you. I am readily available at any given moment. When you call out to Me, I listen. When you come near to Me, I draw near to you. When you sit in my lap, I wrap My arms around you in a loving embrace."

christian bosse

The presence of the storm does not denote the absence of the Lord. His love surpasses all things past, present and future. It flows down from heaven, like a dew of honey. You cannot escape His love. It sticks to you, leaving fresh footprints wherever you go. You are covered in His sweet love and affection. Taste and see that He is good.

thirst

The love of God is like a branch stretching out over you. The waves have carried you off but they have guided you to this place. You can choose to grab a hold of the branch, pulling yourself above the raging waters. Or you can sink down, letting yourself be swallowed up by the surge.

Tightly grasp the love of God. Let Him hold you above the rushing current.

christian bosse

"I say to God my Rock,
    'Why have you forgotten me?'
Why must I go about mourning,
    oppressed by the enemy?
My bones suffer mortal agony
    as my foes taunt me,
saying to me all day long,
    'Where is your God?'"

Psalm 42:9-10 NIV

thirst

christian bosse

The path has led you to this place: a cold, damp cave behind a waterfall. You huddle in a corner, hoping to provide yourself a sense of warmth. You are tired and weary, worn out from the storm. You think, "if only I could wait it out."

The thunder bellows as the rain crashes down even harder than before. It seems as though you're stranded here Will you ever make it out?

thirst

You are not forgotten.
God remembers you.

He is still your Rock.

christian bosse

You are not forsaken. God is here,
calling you out of your darkness,
drawing you near,
giving you a purpose,
and driving out all fear.

You are not forsaken. You are being taken
out of the mire and clay
into a world unknown
that might seem foreign to you today,
but is soon-to-be your home.

You are not forsaken.
God is with you.

thirst

Questions surround you like a thick fog of mystery. Why am I here? Where did these troubles come from? Do I deserve this? Is there a way out? Why am I not seeing the Lord's mighty hand lifting me out of my turmoil?

christian bosse

Though you know the Lord loves you, you look around and feel abandoned. Has He left you here to find your way through the storm? How could He do such a thing?

Little do you know; God's eye is on you. He has not given up.

thirst

The fog of mystery
swirls around my head.
My eyes can barely catch
a glimpse of what's up ahead.
I wander about wondering,
I can't even sleep in my own bed.
My fear has become a protective layer
that I hope to one day shed.
As I look into the fog of mystery,
I try to remember what God has said.

christian bosse

Almighty One,
loving and kind,
with eyes full of peace.
He's one of a kind.

Almighty One,
made of mercy and grace.
You are majestic and wonderful.
If only I could see your face.

Almighty One,
speaking only what is true.
I try to hold on to hope.
I try my best to trust you.

God's character isn't up for debate. It is your choice to recognize His attributes. Nothing you do, say, think or feel subtracts from God's character. Nothing. But how you perceive His actions is solely up to you. When you choose to see God as absent, cruel, and demeaning, you choose to build a wall between you and Him. In doing so, you choose to build a wall between you and His faithfulness, His protection and His provision. You choose to survive the storm alone.

What if you are the one in the way of your breakthrough? What if your decision to see God as malevolent is cutting you off from His benevolence?

christian bosse

You
are only
as strong as
the person or
thing you put your
faith into. Where are you
drawing your strength from today?

"When you rush to make a way where there is no way, you chose to be god of your own life.

I cannot be held accountable for plans I didn't create."

Muster up the courage to put down your own plans. For far too long, you've put yourself before God, choosing your will over His. When you make yourself the source of your sustenance, you choose to experience limited breakthrough. You are only human. You can only do so much. But God is supernatural, all-powerful, all-knowing, and all-sufficient. Lay down your self-security. Allow God to be the source of your strength.

Whether your wounds are self-inflicted or brought on by the storm, submit to God. Choose His authority over your own ideas. He is not malevolent. He is for you. Submit to the plans of the Father. He alone has all you need.

christian bosse

Sometimes, God asks us to do wild things in faith. Do the crazy, unpopular thing He asks of you. Go out on a limb. Don't hesitate to be obedient. Out-of-the-box tasks precede out-of-the-box blessings.

thirst

Mockers dart their eyes to and fro, acting innocent when you're around. Gossips write your headline in secret places, spreading news they never fact-checked.

It might seem that all eyes are on you, anticipating your every move. Stand tall. Draw your strength from the Almighty God, the Rock of your salvation. When they see Him standing behind you, the mockers and gossips will begin to stutter. For every word that rises against you, God condemns.

christian bosse

Stand up. Dust yourself off. Move forward. Your enemies might be taunting you today, but they'll be groveling tomorrow.

thirst

It may look like you're surrounded by enemies, but God stands in the gap.

christian bosse

"Why, my soul, are you downcast?
　　Why so disturbed within me?
Put your hope in God,
　　for I will yet praise Him,
　　my Savior and my God."

Psalm 42:11 NIV

thirst

You might not know how you got here.
That's okay. You aren't meant to look
back and question. You're meant to
face forward and believe.

christian bosse

Train yourself to see blessings all around you, instead of grumbling and complaining. In Christ you're made a victor. It's time to stop playing the victim.

"My beloved, do not worry about the temporary afflictions. Do not exhaust yourself with doubt. I call out to you, "lift up your head!" I did not create you to fear the giants. I am your Father. Don't you know that nothing can stand in the way of My promises to you? Pick up your harp. Ready your trumpet. Go into battle with a shout, for I am the One who fights for you."

christian bosse

Pray.
Worship.
Bow down.
Stay still.

The Lord goes before you.
The battle is already won.

thirst

Do not waste another moment sitting on the sidelines. Get up and follow your Savior into battle.

Nothing can stand in the way of the promises of God. His promises are "yes" and 'amen." All that you have lost will be restored to you. Not in the condition it once was, but in a more glorious state than before. Get ready for an upgrade.

thirst

Say this aloud:

"Captivity cannot hold me any longer. I have been set free. My circumstances might seem bleak, but restoration is coming my way. My God has not left me. He isn't watching me suffer. My God goes before me and wages war on my behalf. It may look like I am in chains, but my Savior has given me the key. I will rise from this place. I know I am free."

christian bosse

The walls aren't caving in.
The sky isn't falling.
Chains are breaking loose.
Barriers are coming down.

thirst

The storm may rage on, but it will come to an end. Your story isn't over. Continue to seek God, no matter how heavy the rain pours. Hope in His unfailing love. Sunshine is on the horizon.

christian bosse

Chase after the Lord
with every last breath.
Let nothing stop you,
not even death.

Chase after God,
whatever you do.
Seek His face.
He will see you through.

Chase after your Savior,
run into His embrace.
He loves you fiercely.
Don't slow your pace.

Chase after the Lord.

thirst

It isn't always easy.
    Sometimes your legs feel like they'll give out.
    But a Voice is calling you.
    It's like a familiar melody.
    You're not going to a foreign place.
        Somehow, you know you're on your way back home.

christian bosse

And now, here we are.
At last, we are at the end.
Are you ready for what's next?
Are you ready to begin?

I pray your mind is open
and that your heart feels a little lighter.
May you see the darkness around you
and know Who makes it brighter.

May your heart never grow dry
and you never feel benched.
Continue to seek the Lord
and never let your heart be quenched.

thirst

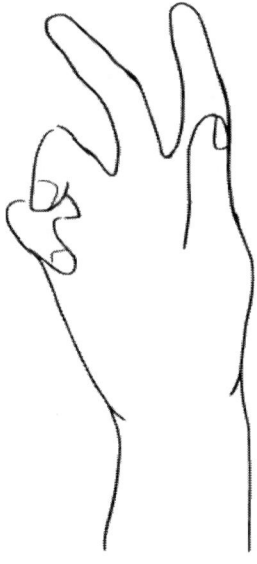

christian bosse

Thirst again.

thirst

christian bosse

about the author

Photo taken by Laura Campbell

Christian Bosse is an American author/poet, mother, and wife. She invites others to find healing and revelation through the power of creativity. Christian leverages her gift of writing and knack for creating to provide a space for others to see their world in a new light, ultimately challenging them to experience peace and growth. Her diverse background in art, counseling, media and faith mix to create a beautiful tapestry of compelling work.

Christian is a Kansas City native, currently residing there with her talented husband and beautiful daughters. When she isn't writing or mentoring, Christian is spending quality time with her family and loved ones.

Christian loves to connect via social media. You can find her on:
Instagram, Pinterest, and Twitter - @christianbosse_
Facebook - @christianbosseofficial

christian bosse

Made in the USA
Monee, IL
19 March 2020